Steps To My True Self

A Self Awareness Guidebook For Youth

By Umm Jasmine Dia

ausetatenra@gmail.com

www.childrenliveon.net

First Edition

Printed in the USA

Steps To My True Self A Self Awareness Guidebook for Youth

By Umm Jasmine Dia

ISBN 9780692817827 paperback

Cover art by Artist Frank Frazier

Proceeds from the sales of Steps To My True Self will benefit the building of Children Live On Exploration & Healing Garden. Thank You.

Inquiries please email: ausetatenra@gmail.com   or visit our website www.childrenliveon.net

Table of Content

Step To A Healthy Me & Self Responsibility

Steps To A Healthy Me & Self Responsibility   Auset Atenra

Message from Auset Maat

Just imagine your identity stolen and your lineage wiped out, you're like a tree cut off from its root. The question is, does this tree have the ability to propagate? Does it carry within its severed self the genetic information that will allow it to regrow a root out of the place where it has been cut off? I believe so. This is the dilemma of the children and people in our world.

With the right knowledge and nurturing these severed trees will once more live and fulfill their purpose. Trusting their intelligent design guiding them to rediscover their own truth and rejecting any false teaching that has been programmed into them. If one lacks self-identity it is difficult to maintain harmony within one's self. I know wellness and balance is vital in sustaining harmony in our lives. Self-Identity is essential for children's growth and development into a Realized Human-Being. Also learning universal laws and wisdom of life is vital.

Children are not learning and applying much wisdom in life. I believe that universal laws need to be incorporated in our lives and taught to children, just like any other laws that govern our world, the universal law governs our lives. Eg "The law of Cause and Effect"- every action has a reaction and follows a chain of events. The choices that we make create the path to our future. We are now the participants of the aftermath of the choices that were made in the past. We are the creators of the future. How will we use this present moment to create the future? Demonstrating this universal law of Cause and Effect. Fundamentally, if we teach children to be well in all areas of their lives Mind Body Spirit Soul, and how to create more things of balance. We will have finally learned how to master our world creating harmony and balance.

Another great universal law is ' The Planting Analogy' The process of planting a seed and the benefit of what you reap is a universal and timeless concept that is a key component for success in our world. . The Planting Analogy explores our purpose and roles that we play. How well we accept life and the roles that we each must play is essential for creating harmony in our lives. We share a symbiotic relationship with all life. The sooner we realize and accept this truth, the more harmonious we will all be. I know that we are each a link in the circle of life and that each link has roles to play in the well being of All children of life, and sustaining the bio diverse community of life. It is our responsibility to maintain that balance. We can achieve balance if we are cultivating balanced minds, nurturing the Self and providing more and better support in helping children through their transitions in life. Ultimately if families, school, and communities join hands; with the knowledge that we are creators with the power to change our circumstances, then the possibilities are endless.

Thank You

Auset Maat

DEDICATION

'Steps To My True Self' A Self Awareness Guide book is dedicated to Saroya, Zenubi, ZoMansour, Livon, Bianca, Lael, Yohan, Aya, Zhinu, Mbwani, Moo Nam, Phoenix. To all little human beings.

May you continue to Be Who You Are. Live your 'TRUTH'. Claim your Sovereignty and attain your liberation. Remember: Your BODY is the temple. It houses your Pure Self. Keep your mind, body pure and in union with Your Pure Self. Remember, you are not your mind. Therefore don't do everything your mind tells you. This mind is impure and delusional. Thanks for being such great teachers.

Special Thanks to William Foeste, Barry Schwartz, Artist Frank Fraiser, Kolongi, LaMetra Martin, My mother self Bromelda Penelope. I thank you.

As I carry the rocks on our back, the stones get smoother;

May the Supreme Self Unmanifest, Infinite Primal Light I One True Pure Self infuse us and Awake our Infinite Potential and Purify us to Rise to the Occasion.

Thank you, Thank You To I Primal Light Parent Self Aten Ra. Much Honor and Reverence To All The I And I Self In Alignment To Restore Balance Back To I One True Pure Self. Victory. Victory.

I Bow To I And I In Self, Light And Truth

Auset Atenra

STEPS TO A HEALTHY ME

&

SELF

RESPONSIBILITY

This is me today!

Date:

Name:_____

Pet name (AKA) _____

Age:___   weight: ___   height:___

Birthday: _____

School: _____ Grade: ____

What do I like about my name?

What do I like best about myself?

What do I like about my family members?

Draw: Self Portrait

Steps To A Healthy Me & Self Responsibility   Auset Atenra

Self-Identity
Who Am I?

Usually when you are asked the question. Who am I? You answer with your name. What's in a name?

Did you know you are more than just your name?

Name:

Who named you?

Why did they choose that name?

What does your name mean?

What is the origin of my name?

What does my name say about me?

What am I made of?

Assignment: Research the origin of your name.   Create a Poem or A Who Am I book, share your book with a friend or your class.

If you had to choose a name for yourself, what would it be? Why?

What am I made Of ?

Cinquain Poem

What Am I Made of ?

1st line 2 syllable   Pure Light

2nd line 4 syllable   Primal Light Self

3rd line 6 syllable   Pure Light Intelligence

4th line 8 syllable   That Can't Be Named, Can't Be Explained

5th line 2 syllable   Self Truth

WRITE YOUR POEM BELOW:

Bio Poem

Write a Biography poem, for each letter of your name write four words that describe you.

(First Name) eg, Auset Maat

Four words that describes you

For example: Auset Maat

A - All, Auset, Atenra, Advercator

U-unique, unity, universal, understanding

DRAW: Who you are and what you are made of.

Steps To A Healthy Me & Self Responsibility   Auset Atenra

Write your I Am Poem here.
I Am………..

Steps To A Healthy Me & Self Responsibility   Auset Atenra

Who Am I?

I am a leader

I am a warrior

I am a good person, I fight for what's right

I don't like the dark so I am the person who leads people to the light

I am the person who cheer people up when they feel down.

I am an eagle mixed up with birds and ant.

I am fierce, I like to soar. I am strong.

I am also a caring person.

I am fearless, but another part of me is not.

I am bold. I am a Goddess.

Zhinu M. 8yrs old

I am Mbwani

I am not who you think I am

I am the wind that follows a certain path

I am the warrior that fights for pride and honor.

I am not your enemy, but the antithesis of that.

I might not be in control of others but I know who I am and this is what makes me unique.

I am an Aries

I am a human being just like the rest

I am not a sin.

I am the future doctor that'll cure toxic disease

I am from the mother land

And yet I act like a civilian here

I haven't forgotten my past,

For that has made me the man of today.

I am the Healer. I am Peace

Mbwani T. 15yrs old

I am Lael Victoria Polius

I am Destiny. I am free.

I am the Earth , Sun and Moon.

I rise above all. I Am One. I Am All.

While other people sleep and dream,   I wake up and work hard.

I do not set low goals for myself just because others look down upon me.

While others fear for the future, I wait till I get to that bridge to cross it.

I am a Goddess. I Am the One Most High.

I am Light. I am Bright.

I face danger without hesitation.

I am brave. I am strong.

I am the face of all Life.

I AM ME!

-Lael Victoria Polius 9yrs old

I am strong as an elephant

I sting like a bee

I came from the mother land

I am like a key

I came as a purpose

Purpose of what life to be

The question is, Who Am I?

I found out I Am Me!

I am who I want to be

-   Moo Nam 11 yrs old

I AM ...

I am Phoenix

I am a Soccer player

I am smart. I am like a Dolphin

I like Sharks and Fish

I encourage others

I am Phoenix

- Phoenix K. 7yrs old

I am a generous person

And a person who loves

I do not deny love

I will not disregard love

I do not kill love and

I do not kill living things

-Yohan P. 6yrs old

Who Am I?

You are not who you think you are

Asking 'Who Am I ' is the best place to start

You are more than your name, body and mind

More than your Life circumstances at this time

You are an intelligent Design

Ask yourself daily "Who Am I's"

Now watch as your intelligence climb

You have been on this journey for many life times

"Who Am I" before the beginning of Time?

Who Am I after the body decline?

Ignorance of "The True Self" is the worst crime

Know Thy Self and change the paradigm

The inward 'I' must triumph over Mind

Seek the initial 'I' , who will lead you to The I "One
True Pure Self. I seek To Know Who Am I?

Auset Atenra

Who Am I?

Who Am I?

Don't let others define you 'who you are'. Seek that knowing and experience yourself. You must experience yourself to know your truth.

Think for a moment the marvelous transformation taking place at your conception; from a tiny egg and sperm into a human being. Who is the maker of this body? What is this Intelligence?

To me it's quite obvious that no outside force, no doctors, humans are conducting this amazing miraculous event of sperm and egg into human being,

Then why do we think after we are born others know best? We think we know everything and trust others to define who we are. Why are we not curious about our existence? Why do we just blindly follow the bandwagon? Why do we not ask the intelligence that is working from within?

Life is a precious gift with a limited time to use it. I say Live boldly with Purpose, Be Curious, Ask Questions,. Know Thyself. There is only one way to know thyself is to ask the intelligence that creates and resides in the body. The intelligence that is keeping your heart beating, keeping the breath of life.

Who Am I?

BODY AWARENESS

- Practicing Body Awareness –

- Let's Just be aware of our body and any sensations we are feeling.

- Let's Focus and bring some awareness to our body, relax our body and bring our attention to the different parts of our body. (close eyes – Bring awareness to our brain, ears, mouth, hands, organs etc.

- What are you aware of? How are you feeling? Rub your hands together. What do you Feel?

- Let's bring awareness to our breath. Consciously zone in on our inhalation and exhalation. How am I breathing?

- Continue Practicing BODY AWARENESS . Then see if you can be aware of the energies inside you and around you.

- Lets Focus only on our Breath as we become aware of our surroundings. Can you feel the sensations inside of you and also around you?

- **How are you feeling?**

Conscious Breathing

Breathe In with your whole body.

Then hold your Breath – Observe what happens next

Now, Exhale through your whole body. (Observe what happens next)

(Repeat eight times) 8X

Breath Awareness

"This moment is inevitable. I live with pure self awareness, conscious breath, pure Conscious Thoughts, Words and Action."

Observing My Breath (8X)

1st . Inhale and exhale through nose,

Observe: what happens as a result?

2nd . Inhale through nose,

Exhale through mouth

3rd . Inhale through the whole body,

hold breath, then observe what happen.

4th. Exhale through the whole body.

Observe what happens as a result?

SELF SUFFICIENCY

It is time for us to move to self sufficiency.

I am Self Sufficient. I am All That I Need.

I am equipped with All that I need.

I restore my Light. I restore my balance

I Am That I Am. I Am All. All Is Myself.

BREATH AWARENESS

We are cut off from our "True Self" and one very true way we can connect and have the best awareness of "Who We are is through "Stillness" and bringing awareness to our "Breath". In stillness we can better still the outer noises and make union with our Inner Truth and Self Awareness.

Sit in the lotus position, hands open and resting on knees.

Let's bring awareness to our breath. Inhale ---Exhale   (8X)

How am I breathing?

Now, place your hands on your heart. Can you feel the vibration of your heart?

Can you live without the beating of your heart?

* Chant*   A H– HU M

STILLNESS CHALLENGE

Let's take a moment to practice stillness.

This is a perfect time to ask "Who Am I? Why am I Here?

I challenge you my friend to a game of "STILLNESS".

How long can I sit in stillness for?

Please time yourself.

WHY SHOULD I PRACTICE STILLNESS?

I realize my mind Sometimes tells me to do things that are not right and balanced. I practice Stillness to be calm and balanced.

I practice Stillness to purify my mind.
I practice Stillness to dissolve the ego.
I dissolve this ego.
I say.

"Mind Be Still. Be Still. (2X)
Mind Be Still And Know That I Am In Command. I am in command of my mind.
I Am The Self. You Are The Mind.
I Am Not This Body.
I Am Not This Mind.
Mind Be Still. I am in command of my mind
I Am In Command. Ah Hum, Ah So Hum

What questions do you have?

What would you like to know about life?

Steps To A Healthy Me & Self Responsibility   Auset Atenra

Steps To A Healthy Me & Self Responsibility Auset Atenra

Self Awareness

What is self-awareness?

Self Awareness is.........

How can self-awareness help me in my self-development?

Affirmation: (say 3x)

Being self-aware is a way of life. I am aware of my thoughts, my feelings, and my surroundings. I will better see the effect they have on my emotions, and my actions. Being self aware will help me to practice Stillness and I can choose the right and appropriate Thoughts, Words and Actions.

self-awareness is helping me to understand my actions and reactions and how I respond to life situations.

I am practicing Self Awareness. I am being aware of my thoughts, my words, feelings and my actions.

How many creative ways can I express myself?

Draw your feelings:

Steps To A Healthy Me & Self Responsibility   Auset Atenra

For seven days practice being more self-aware:

How can this awareness help me in being more harmonious and making good choices? How can I be present in this moment?

Self Awareness	Day 1	Day 2	Day 3
Thoughts			
Emotions (my sensing Energy fields)			
Feelings			
Words			
Actions			

Day 4	**Day 5**	**Day 6**	**Day 7**

Steps To A Healthy Me & Self Responsibility   Auset Atenra

My Story:

What do you think about self-awareness? Is it a useful tool in helping one with their self-development?

How has practicing self-awareness helped me?

Steps To A Healthy Me & Self Responsibility

Being Aware of my Challenges and Likes:

Challenges	likes	dislikes
What challenges do I face right now?	What are the things I like?	What are the things I dislike?

Draw:

Memories

What is my first memory?

Draw:

Steps To A Healthy Me & Self Responsibility   Auset Atenra

What is the funniest moment of my life?

Draw:

What do I like to do for fun?

Draw:

Steps To A Healthy Me & Self Responsibility   Auset Atenra

How can I get better at the things I do?

Draw:

What are my favorite things?

Steps To A Healthy Me & Self Responsibility   Auset Atenra

Draw:

Steps To A Healthy Me & Self Responsibility   Auset Atenra

What makes me feel happy, and good inside?

Draw:

Steps To A Healthy Me & Self Responsibility   Auset Atenra

Who are my Best friends? (why?).

Draw:

How do I resolve conflicts with my friends? Why do I?

How do I help out at home, school, and in my community?

Draw:

Draw:

Draw a picture of a memory that is special to you.

WHAT'S IMPORTANT TO ME?

My personal values chart below: Please add more of your personal values and rate them from: Highest importance to least importance of 4 being the highest and 1 being the least.

My Personal Values Chart	4 – Highest Importance	3	2	1-Least Importance
Eating healthy food				
Spending time with family				
Being with friends				
Wearing expensive clothes				
Making good grades				
Finding my purpose in life				
Being popular				
Making good choices				
Being successful in life				
Being Happy and balanced				
Helping others in need				

DRAW: These are the things that are important to me.

Steps To A Healthy Me & Self Responsibility   Auset Atenra

Values & Beliefs

If we understand our beliefs and our values we have a better grip on our behavior and attitudes towards life. Our values and beliefs determine our actions or inaction.

What is the difference between beliefs and values?

Beliefs are our perceptions on life; our thoughts and ideas that we assume are true even if we have no proof.
Values are the things that are significant to us. They are important.

Our beliefs are the driving force behind our values

What are my beliefs and values in life?

Beliefs	Why

Values	**Why**

Eg. You value your social life, hanging out with your friends, you go to school only to socialize and be mischievous. You go to school only because you are forced to.

Many people believe school is boring, and a waste of time. How can a school experience provide an opportunity to acquire knowledge and skills that will help you succeed in life. How can we change the school system to be more balanced meeting the needs of families and the community?

Do you think you can learn how to harness your talents and learn skills for self-development? What can be done to create a better system of education?

Can you find the things that you are interested in and learn it well?

Seek and you shall find.

Word Is Power - Word Is The Mind:

How can I use the "Power of Words" - The "Power of Mind" to create a life that is in alignment with my "Life's Purpose" and my "Self Purpose"?

Remember!!! Be mindful of the thoughts and the words you use. All the creation stories tell us the world was created from THOUGHTS & WORDS. From the thoughts the words were spoken and things came into being.

Look around and see all the things human beings have created; first there was a thought, then came the words, after that came the action. Now behold all the creation of humanity!

How do I use my power of mind to create?

Words Have Power!

Using cuss words and profanity is a norm in today's society, how do you express yourself in words? What are your thoughts on children using so much profanity?

Please choose your words wisely.

Curbing My Mind

For the next two weeks monitor your mind to weed out destructive thoughts and habits.

Life Situations	MY Thoughts	MY Words	MY Action
Eg. Reprimanded by parents	I can't stand my parents...	Cuss word Profanity	Slam room door. Argue a lot

Curbing My Mind

Imagine our mind is under a spell or hypnosis, it brings into our world the things that have been pre program into it. Once we come into awareness we break the spell or hypnosis and now we can with self awareness reprogram our mind to align with our True Self Purpose.

Replacing bad habits with new good habits. Replacing destructive words and actions with healing words and actions.

Life Situations	Positive Thoughts	Healing Words	Healing Actions
Reprimanded by parents	That's a parents POV, point of view	I respect your views, but I would also like you to listen to my views?	Thanks. I will take it into consideration. (Politely close door) clean room.

What am I creating with my thoughts, words and action?

Draw things you would like your mind to bring into your life.

Steps To A Healthy Me & Self Responsibility   Auset Atenra

My Thoughts Create My Life

My action dictates my Thoughts

The way that I think about something determines my actions. Sometimes I have to change my beliefs so that I can have better experiences in life. At other times I have to change my behavior to change my thinking about how I deal with life situations.

How Can I challenge myself to be more self aligned and see things as they are?

How can I analyze the situation to see what I have control over?

What thoughts, words and/or action will I express on this matter?

Steps To A Healthy Me & Self Responsibility

To Do:

Tell of a time when you or someone you know had to change your thinking or behavior about something so you could have a better experience in life.

Change my thinking change my MIND
"Change My action Change my life"

Write a script, then video shoot a commercial 15 sec to 30 seconds long. Use the above saying as the theme

Submit your video on www.childrenliveon.net

Training My Mind

In the beginning was Thoughts. Your thoughts are the Mind. The human body is dormant without the Spirit animating it. The Mind is Powerful.

The working of the MIND is like the workings of a magnet. A magnet is polarized to attract anything iron, cobalt, or nickel and repel another magnet with the same polarity that is trying to take over its magnetic power. Likewise we must polarize our MINDS to attract positive thoughts and things that are in balance and harmony with our Self purpose and life purpose. We want to polarize our minds so it can build our life here in harmony and balance in the things we desire to achieve by programming the mind on what to attract and what to repel. Remember, many thoughts will come, good and bad, negative and positive. Similar to a magnet in the midst of many things, yet the magnet will only attract the things of iron, and repel its same side. Therefore we must polarize our mind to bring into our world balance, harmonic and positive thoughts, words and creations. Like a magnet the mind will repel other minds trying to interfere with its polarization, We must protect our mind from interference and program it to repel other thoughts trying to take it over.

We use our mind to bring things from the mental and spiritual world into our physical world. The mind will not be able to attract something if it is not polarized properly. Also the synopsis in our brain must be able to transfer information and build new brain cells if there are no brain cells available to receive this information. Other times the mind might lack the skills to utilize the information and transfer them adequately to the brain. But if the mind is in awareness with 'True Self' and is balanced, the mind has the ability to convey all information accurately to the brain and spark new brain cells to learn this information if it's needed. Then it will manifest into our physical world. We have to learn to use the Mind to our advantage so the Mind doesn't turn against us. Training the Mind to work effectively for you. **How to cultivate my Mind?**

REMEMBER: With the mind we create our life situations. The mind is the master of manifestation. Remember to practice discernment. How am I cultivating my mind?

Who or what is controlling my mind?

How can I train my Mind to work effectively for me?

Am I in command of my Mind?

"Mind Be still and know that I Am In Command"

WHO OR WHAT IS CONTROLLING MY MIND?

Affirmation say (8X)

I polarize my mind to attract only thoughts, ideas,

Creations in harmony and balance with my Self Purpose and Life Purpose

I create the Brain Cells necessary to receive and utilize this information.

I repel any other thoughts/minds trying to interfere or take over my mind.

I am in command of the commandment command. (8X)

Training My Mind To :

❖ STAY ALERT

❖ STAY STILL WITHOUT THOUGHTS

❖ SELF ALIGN

❖ ILLUMINATE

❖ BE PURE

Please create a black dot, place it 1 ½ ft away from your face. Then stare at the dot without blinking or moving for 15-30 minutes. Don't let thoughts come into your Mind.

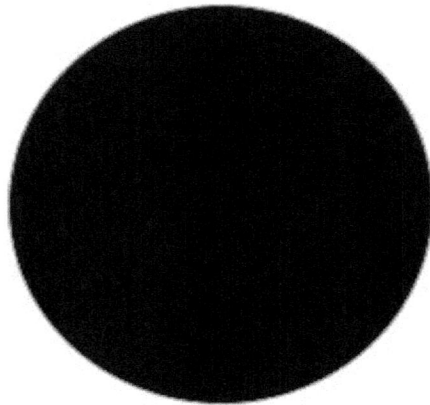

What did you experience doing this mind exercise?

What are some things in our culture that influences our mind? How does it do it?

Draw a picture of how you think the Mind is:

Please finish this sentence.

My mind is……..

I Watch my words, I Watch my mind

I Monitor my thoughts, I Monitor my mind

I Watch my action, I monitor my action

How can I train my Mind?

DAILY STILLNESS CHALLENGE
*Chant - A-U-M (8X)

*Now sit outside in nature with feet touching the Earth.

*Sit in Stillness:

*Recite - "I am Stillness without Thoughts. I Am Calm. I Am Pure.

How long can I sit in stillness for?

Strength and Weakness

Understanding our strengths and weaknesses will help us to strengthen our weaknesses and use our strength to propel us forward in our lives.

Monitoring my strength and weaknesses

Strength

Strength (Write your strengths here)	How can I use my strength to better my life?

Weakness:

Weaknesses	How can I improve my Weakness

SELF-RESPONSIBILITY

What is Self Responsibility?

What are my responsibilities to myself?

As I grow older I will be assign new responsibilities:

When I was _____years old I was not allowed to

_____

_____

_____

_____

_____

_____.

Now that I am ___years old my new responsibilities are

_____

_____

_____

_____.

Affirmation (say 2x)

I have the ability to respond. I respond with Self Awareness. I respond with Conscious thoughts, conscious words and conscious action.

I am responsible for my happiness and for maintaining my balance.

I am responsible for my own education. Knowledge is Freedom

I am responsible for my self-care, using proper hygiene and eating healthy.

I am responsible for my well being, my life. I am responsible.

I take ownership of this power for my self-responsibility.

WHAT STEPS WILL I TAKE TO BE MORE RESPONSIBLE?

Steps To A Healthy Me & Self Responsibility   Auset Atenra

Leadership & Self Responsibility Tips

Michael Bland Principal (Barack Obama Male Leadership Academy)

Use these Tips as an affirmation: **Repeat Daily**

- o I will set High Expectations
- o I will Find a Safe Haven and an environment where education is valued.
- o I will Learn how to prioritize what's important to me
- o I will practice Looking at the consequences of my actions and my choices before I make them.
- o I will choose choices that will not be detrimental to me.
- o Knowing my value system will help me navigate through difficult choices.
- o I will participate in extracurricular activities.
- o Goal Setting will allow me to stay on track
- o I will learn life lessons from the people and the environment around me.
- o I see equity in my education, my education is an investment in my future

"When you empower children in who they are and what role they play in the instruction and learning that take place their leadership qualities start to come out. Let's provide children with a strong family structure in the home, school and community."

Michael Bland (Principal)

Barack Obama Male Leadership Academy

Steps To A Healthy Me & Self Responsibility   Auset Atenra

Self –Discipline

What is self Discipline?

TO DO:

How can self-discipline help me in my self-development?

Affirmation

Being self discipline is a sign of maturity. I have the ability and will power to motivate myself in spite of any negative Feelings or thoughts. I will be persistent and I will work hard to achieve my goals.

I take ownership of this power to be self-disciplined.

I am Self Discipline

Self Control

What is Self Control?

Our behavior is determined by how we are feeling. Our thoughts and feelings determine our actions.

Self-Control

If I Don't Control myself, someone else or a system will control me. It's not always easy to Master our Feelings and Balance our Mind.

Self Control can help me in how I express my feelings and redirect my thoughts.

I can take responsibility for my Feelings and thoughts by being aware of how I am feeling and what thoughts I am thinking. My Action is my responsibility, I balance my mind. I make good choices.

If I listen to my heart beating then I am able to calm myself down and choose the right action. My Actions are in alignment with my One True Pure Self.

Healthy self-expression is a sign of maturity. I express myself through poems, music, meditation, yoga, being in nature, art and other positive mediums.

I AM THE MASTER OF MY Feelings And Mind.

TO DO:

How can self-Control help me in my self-development?

Tell of a time when self-control was necessary in your life.

Draw:

Steps To A Healthy Me & Self Responsibility   Auset Atenra

Affirmation

I am the master of my feelings. Emotions are our Electrical Sensing Fields of Energy that permeate inward and outward the realm of our body. It is interpreting our inner world and outer world and sending signals to our Mind/Brain/Body. Chemicals that trigger feelings and emotions are also created in the brain. The way that I feel about something triggers an emotion.

If I change the way that I feel and think about something I can master my emotion. If I practice Emotional Awareness and change the way I feel about something. I can master my mind.

I Take ownership of this Power to be Self Controlled.'

He who conquers ego self is the mightiest warrior.

I AM THE MASTER OF MY FEELINGS & MIND

Out of My Control

Cause and Effect will set in motion many chains of action and reaction, then more causes and more effects. Many things will happen in life that we will not have any control over. Sometimes in life things happen that are out of our control. There are many forces at play intertwining for life's happenings. Therefore things don't always work out the way we envision or plan.

 How do I deal with life's disappointments?

What do I do when things don't work out the way I planned?

I have learned to respond to life disappointments with these questions.

First:

Q. What do I have control over?

A. I have control over my action, my thoughts. How I think about this situation.

I have control over the words I will use to analyze and observe this situation.

I have control over my actions. How I choose to respond to the situation. What I do next will set off another chain of reaction of causes and effects.

NEXT:

How am I going to respond to my next question? Then I move into the direction of what thoughts will I entertain? What will my words and actions be? After I receive my answers to these questions, I proceed to accomplish and focus my mind on the things that I have control over.

THEN:

I move into the direction of the things I have control over. I focus my mind in the present Moment to the task at hand. Now, at this moment. I command my mind to build mental stamina. I proceed with confidence and certainty to the things I have control over.

How can these steps to handle disappointment help us in our life journey? How will these Steps be of help to you?

Other Elements at Play

Sometimes one has done everything in one's power that one needed to do but unfortunately one didn't get the result one was aiming for. Things didn't work out the way we planned.

I realize that this was another test from life. I also remember that life is a school for me to learn about duality.

Due to duality, we live in a world where good and bad exist. Light and darkness, Ego and Self etc. Life is always going to test to see if I have mastered my lessons. So I realize that these disappointments were also a test to see if I could be okay regardless of the outcome.

Could I lose attachment to ideas, things and just be self aware?

Can I be in the moment, and be at peace?

Can I maintain harmony and balance?

Can I be pleasant within myself regardless of my external situations?

What life lessons am I learning?

Daily Practice

REMEMBER:

THIS IS THE MOMENT!

- ✔ BE PRESENT IN THE MOMENT
- ✔ STAY ALERT
- ✔ STAY IN SELF ALIGNMENT
- ✔ STAY STILL WITHOUT THOUGHTS
- ✔ SMILE – IT'S LIFE GAME
- ✔ CONSCIOUS BREATHING
- ✔ STAY VIGILANT AGAINST THE MIND
- ✔ TAKE COMMAND
- ✔ STAY CALM AND COMPOSE

I am alert.
I am awake.
I am calm.

Healthy Self Expression

Choosing how to express ourselves helps us to bring our creativity to the world. When we have strong feelings and thoughts we can choose to express them in healthy ways. Healthy self-expression helps us in our self-development and our maturity of ourselves. Healthy Self Expression also helps us in choosing the Right Action and creative ways to express ourselves.   We can show anger in art, song, poem, cooking, painting, dance etc...

How do I express myself?

How many creative ways can I express myself?

DRAW:

Draw your expressions of different feelings.
Which is your favorite Feeling?

Identifying Thoughts and Feelings

I will start to identify my thoughts, and feelings, and the many different ways I express myself in my daily life.

What are the patterns and cycles of my thoughts and feelings?

Things	How I view them	Thoughts and feelings	Patterns And Cycles **Cause & Effect** What triggers these thoughts & feelings?	How can I change my thoughts & feelings to create harmony?

Feeling & Emotions

What are emotions?

What are feelings?

"

Emotions are our Electrical Sensing Fields of energy. It is a heightened sense of awareness that extends inward and outward of the realm of our body.

It can pick up sensations we are not aware of and then it feeds them into the brain, the brain sends signals to our body, based on our previous programing of our mind. We will react based on that sensation. Sometimes we don't fully understand the emotions we are feeling. Our interpretations and expressions might reflect the contrary.

Chemicals that trigger emotions are also created in the brain. The way that I feel about something triggers an emotion. If I change my thoughts and feelings I can master my emotions. If I practice emotional awareness then I can learn the triggers, and understand when I have an overwhelming emotion to pause and meditate on the root cause and the road to healing.

We have to try to get to the root of the feeling and thoughts, only then can we be free and be healed. Why am I feeling and thinking this way? Only then will we become the masters of our emotions

What is the root cause of this thought and feeling?

What lessons do I need to learn?

Sacred Circle Meditation

Creating a sacred circle is vital to helping us in our healing and identifying our feelings and thoughts and bringing balance to them.

REMEMBER: In your sacred circle it is just you and you alone. Put yourself in your self healing circle and listen to your inner truth and inner wisdom. Everything and everyone stays outside of your sacred circle.

The more we practice the better we'll be at balancing and mastering our feelings and thoughts. We will find creative ways to express ourselves.

Practice the meditation below daily.

Sacred Circle Song

Putting my sacred circle on (2x)

Light bright like the Sun, encircle me all around

Primal Light, I Am That I Am

I am in alignment with I One True Pure Self.

I am healed. I am healed.

From head to toe; Crankiness, sickness.

You got to go. My Mind is alert and focused.

I'm Ready for the task at hand

My Mind is Still without thoughts.

Inhale I breathe. Exhale I release.

I am healed. I am healed.

After doing your Daily Sacred Circle Meditation; what did you learn about yourself?

Feelings are dominant forces in our lives. our emotions are real. We interpret our emotions through our feelings. Our feelings give voice to our emotions. Our emotions can trigger a feeling and vice versa. We act on that feeling. We express ourselves based on our feelings. Therefore our feelings dictate our life.

The law of attraction says whatever we think about the most. We bring that reality into our lives, even the things that we don't want.

I create my life out of my thoughts and feelings.

Affirmation (2X)

I will meditate on what I need daily?

I am in awareness of my thoughts, my feelings, my emotions. I acknowledge the way that I feel. I look at the root cause of my thoughts, my feelings, and emotions. Now I can heal and choose the right and appropriate response to my thoughts, feelings and emotions.

THINGS (It's not the things that upsets us)	How I View THING (It's the way we view them that upsets us)

Steps To A Healthy Me & Self Responsibility   Auset Atenra

Wants VS Needs: Please write your wants and needs

Wants I can live without it	Need necessary for life

Freedom Taken Away

If I Don't Control myself, someone else or a system will control me. I am self governing.

Tell of a time when your freedom was taken away. What were the cause and the effect?

How did you handle the situation?

Remember: It's a test, it's like building a bridge. How will I know my bridge is strong enough to cross?   It will be tested. I will be tested.

This is a test,
This is a test
This is a test
Stay Strong

Be on guard

Affirmation (say 3X)

I recognize that feelings are a way of life. I am perfecting myself in the feelings of unconditional Love, Compassion, Caring, Harmlessness and Forgiveness. I balance all my karma from this and past lives. I speak my Truth, I live my self Truth. I live in balance and harmony.

Steps To A Healthy Me & Self Responsibility

TO DO: What is personal freedom?

What happens to people when their personal freedom is taken away?

PERSONAL FREEDOM TAKEN AWAY

Research cases of people in our culture whose personal freedom has been taken away, maybe they are incarcerated or in a mental institution.   What choices lead to their freedom being taken away?

Do you think that it was just cause?

Steps To A Healthy Me & Self Responsibility   Auset Atenra

SELF PRESERVATION

What is Self Preservation?

Research to see if you can find people who practice self-preservation. How can SELF PRESERVATION help you to preserve your essence and live life harmoniously following your Self Purpose and your Life purpose?

Affirmation

I am practicing self-preservation. I am preserving my Essence.
I embrace Food, people, things, thoughts and actions that
promote Life balance and harmony. I banish sickness, disease,
self-destruction from my sacred circle. I am beyond this body.
I am beyond this Mind.

I Am That I Am. I am awake. I am All. I Am Light.

To Do:

Write a persuasive speech: Why is it important to preserve our lives? Why are the 'the Guiding Principles of self' important? How can "The Guiding Principles of Self" help one to avoid negative choices and life paths?

.   Submit you speech on

www.childrenliveon.net

Memorize the **"Guiding Principles of Self"**

Brainstorm your ideas here!

Thesis statement: Topic Sentence

Introduction:

Main Idea 1: Supporting details

Main Idea 2: Supporting details

Main Idea 3: Supporting details

Conclusion:

Writing 1st Draft:

Steps To A Healthy Me & Self Responsibility   Auset Atenra

Guiding Principles of Self

I _____ _is thriving for Self-responsibility, Self-mastery, self-awareness, self-identity, self-preservation, self-discipline, self control, self-innovation and self-actualization.

SELF-RESPONSIBILITY: I have the ability to respond with Self Conscious Awareness. Conscious breath, thoughts, words and actions. I am responsible for my actions, my life , my education, my health, and my wealth.

SELF-MASTERY-   I am that I Am. I Am that I will be.   In this awareness I know my given skills, knowledge and abilities. I utilize them appropriately.

SELF-AWARENESS: I am mindful of my thoughts, words, feelings, and actions. My thoughts, my words, my feelings, and my actions create my reality. I Am Pure Light.

SELF-PRESERVATION: I strive to maintain balance of mind, body, and self. I protect myself from destructive and negative thoughts and words, food that promotes premature death. I thrive on actions that promote longevity. Life is for living. I Am alive. I live in harmony and balance with my One True Pure Self.

SELF-IDENTITY: I practice "Who Am I Self Inquiry" Meditation so I can know who I am for myself. I Must know for myself who I am.   I Am All. I must realize that All is myself. I express myself through nature. I express my Authentic Self .I am That I Am. I Am That Has No Name. I Am That Can't Be Explained.

SELF-DISCIPLINE: I check and manage my own behavior, therefore, someone else or a system won't discipline or manage me. I Am in command of my mind and my body.

SELF-CONTROL: I am the master of my feelings and mind. He who conquers ego self is the mightiest warrior. My actions are my karma. I am in command. Mind Be Still. I Am the Self.

SELF-INNOVATION: I am a creator, creating. I use my creative power to create with my thoughts, my words, my hands, my actions and my knowledge. What are my thoughts creating me? What will my hand's creation be? What will my footprints leave?

SELF ACTUALIZATION: Be Who I Am. I am Primal Light. All Is Myself. I Am One With All. I am balanced. I Am That I Am. . I Am That. I am self aligned with I One True Pure Self.

 SELF-LOVE: I Love myself enough to connect to my inner Truth and live from that awareness.   I live my best life in equanimity and harmony. .   I Am That I Am.

Steps To A Healthy Me & Self Responsibility

Habits

What are habits?

Good habits VS bad habits

Write below examples of good and bad habits...

GOOD HABITS	BAD HABITS

Habits are easily formed but hard to break. Throughout your life remember to form good habits.

To do:

Research habits in your community and identify the effect of these habits. Tell us why it is important to formulate good habits.

Steps To A Healthy Me & Self Responsibility   Auset Atenra

My Hygiene

What is hygiene?

How can I practice proper hygiene?

How does poor hygiene affect one's self esteem and the people around them?

Steps To A Healthy Me & Self Responsibility   Auset Atenra

SELF CARE CHART

My Body	Proper Hygiene (what is the best way of taking care of my teeth?)	Poor Hygiene	Consequences of poor hygiene (What happens if I don't?)
Teeth			
Face			
Hair			
Nails			
Feet			
Body			
Clothes			

Daily Schedule

Time	Activity/chore

Weekly:

Monthly:

Health

Food and nutrition are essential to the structures of the Body's DNA. Our environment can also affect and change our genetic structure. Food can change the structure of our DNA. Food engineering can destroy our DNA so our body's defense against proper nutrition is being compromised. We have the ability to tap into information stored within us so we can master our journey here and be prepared to leave when it is time to go. Yes, food and things engineered today can interrupt our ability to connect to our inner Truth to be who we are and live our life purpose and Self Purpose.

Research food being engineered and the process it goes through versus food growing wild naturally without the interference of man and their pesticides and fertilizer.

Eg. Jicama versus Breadfruit and corn :

Coconut oil VS canola oil. What is canola oil? What are the ingredients and processes to make canola oil? What are the ingredients and processes in making coconut oil?

To Do:

How can I choose healthy choices when I am bombarded with numerous choices of food and things that promote premature death and self-destruction?

Healthy Mind, Body and Self

What do I need to create a healthy mind, body and self?

BODY	MIND	SPIRIT

Our Mind can affect our DNA. Did you know the thoughts we think create changes in our body and cells?

Conduct a Research on this idea.

NUTRITION

What is nutrition and how does one benefit from nutrition?

What kind of nutrition do I need to live a balanced righteous life?

Draw two columns below one with a list of Food that promotes premature death VS food that promotes longevity.

Affirmation (say 3x)

I keep my body clean I shower and purify

I keep my thoughts and mind clean, clear and positive

I keep my self in union with my ultimate PURE SELF TRUTH. I am purifying my space and energy

I cleanse myself of destructive habits, thoughts and belief systems. My thoughts and beliefs are in unison with my true purpose and One True Pure Self.

I have the ability to respond. I respond with Self Awareness.

I respond with Righteous thoughts, words and action.

I am responsible for my happiness, and my balance

I am responsible for my own education. Self Knowledge is freedom and power. I thrive to know my PURE True Self.

I am responsible for my self care, brushing my teeth, using proper hygiene, I am responsible for the food I consume into my body.

Being responsible is a sign of maturity. I own this power to Self-Responsibility.

I AM RESPONSIBLE.

Draw:

Steps To A Healthy Me & Self Responsibility   Auset Atenra

Nutrition Chart

Food	Nutritional value	Natural food (Is it natural?)	Man-made engineer crop (Is it man made?)

Blessing My Food

I bless this food, this liquid. Provide me the nutrient and energy I need to repair, rejuvenate and to promote longevity.   I give thanks to all the elements that came together to bring it into being.

Thank You, Thank You,   (2X)

Affirmation

My Body is A Sacred Temple

Inside & outside the box

Hexahedron

Copy this hexahedron onto a sheet of copy paper, then cut it out to make a cube

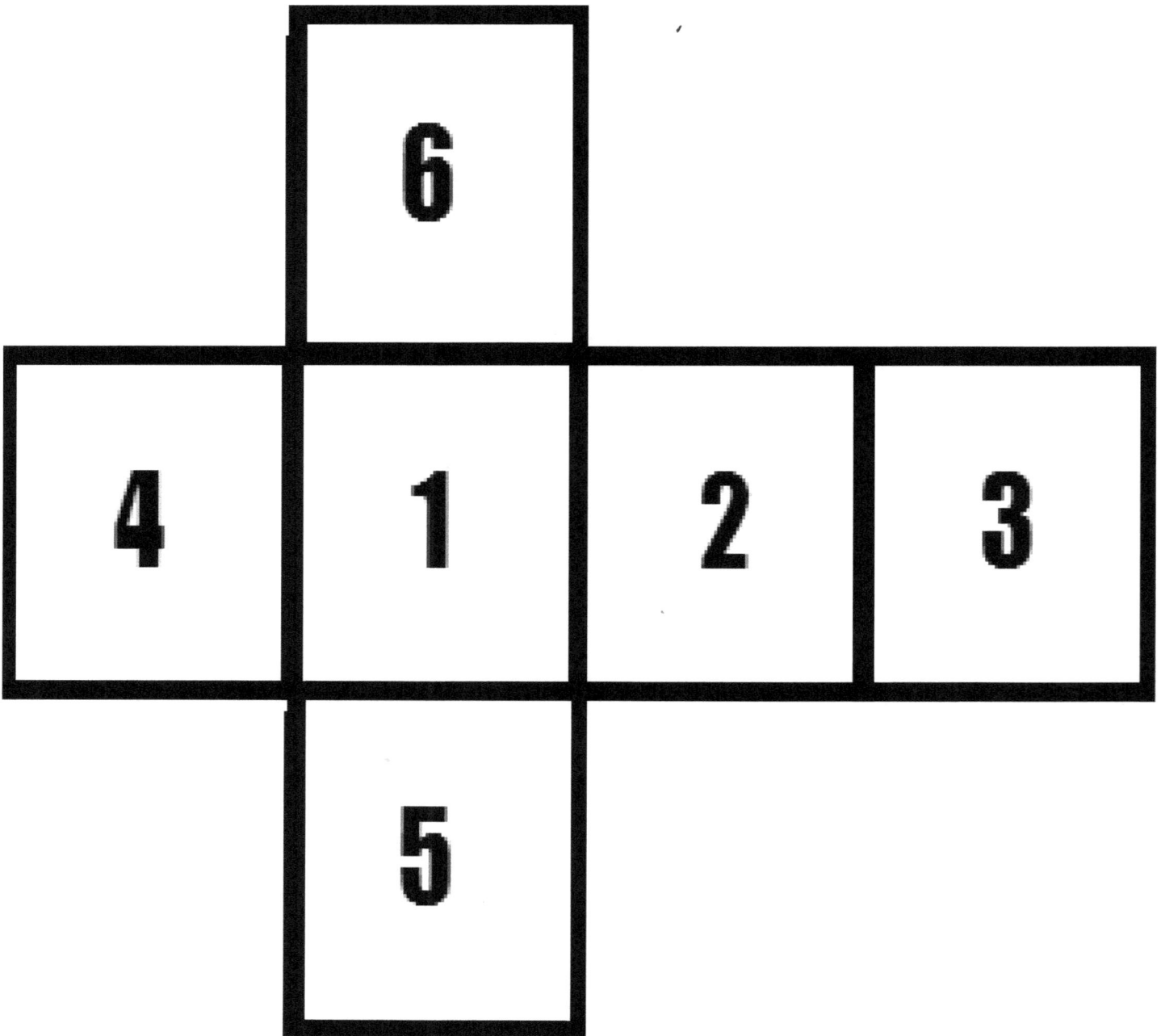

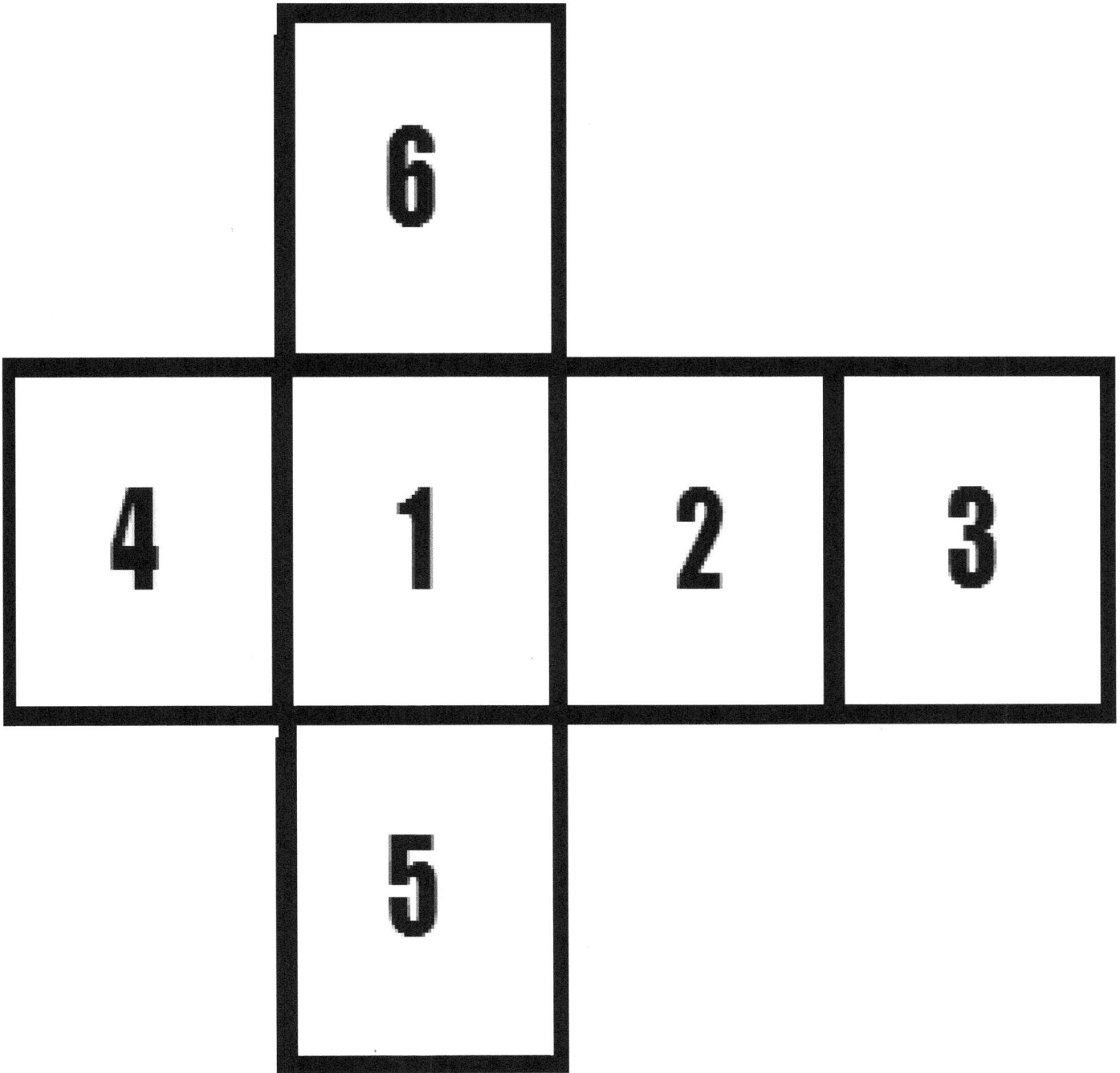

		6	
4	1	2	3
		5	

Steps To A Healthy Me & Self Responsibility

Steps To A Healthy Me & Self Responsibility

Steps To A Healthy Me & Self Responsibility

Inside & Outside the Box

WHO DO YOU THINK I AM?

How would the following people describe me?

How do others see me?

Parent 1.

Grand
Parents:

Siblings:

How do I
See My
Self?

Parent 2:

How do others see me?

Neighbors:

Best Friends:

Other Friends:

How Do
I See
Myself?

Teachers:

Mirror Mirror

When I look in the mirror, who do I see?

How can I see my True Self?

Draw: Reflection of My-Self

AUTOGRAPH: Have family, teachers and friends sign your book with advice or compliment.

Steps To A Healthy Me & Self Responsibility   Auset Atenra

AUTOGRAPH: Have family, teachers and friends sign your book with advice or compliment.

My Heritage

MY Family History

Find out more about your heritage. Create a display and chart a timeline. family tree, journal entries, a story, or a collection of photographs, artifacts about your culture/ethnic heritage.

"Out Of Many We Are One". Out of One Came Many"

Time Capsule

Create a time capsule and tell why the objects you have chosen to put into your time capsule are important to you.

Steps To A Healthy Me & Self Responsibility   Auset Atenra

MY HERITAGE

CULTURE HERITAGE
Diversity is what makes the world so beautiful and colorful. From one source we see myriads of creation. How boring life would be if we didn't have diversity. Be proud of your heritage. Out of One came many. Out of many, we are one.

The African connection; could you trace your heritage back to Africa, Europe, Asia, or any other culture? Watch the -Film- tracing my roots

Find out about your lineage.
Interview people of different ages and backgrounds to find out what it was like when they were growing up? Compare the similar and different concerns you have about growing up.

"Out Of Many We Are One". Out of One Came Many"

Interview people who share your heritage to find out what challenges they faced when they were your age?

What were their hopes and dreams?

What do they deem their great accomplishment?

My Family Tree

Fam·i·ly Tree

Noun

1. A diagram showing the relationships between people in several generations of a family.

2. All of the descendants and ancestors in a family.

Synonyms

pedigree - lineage - genealogy - heritage - stemma

My Family Tree

Steps To A Healthy Me & Self Responsibility   Auset Atenra

Create a family collage: Go get your family to help you design this page

Steps To A Healthy Me & Self Responsibility   Auset Atenra

AUTOGRAPH: Have family and friends sign your book

Steps To A Healthy Me & Self Responsibility   Auset Atenra

AUTOGRAPH: Have family and friends sign your book

Socialization:

Socialization is the interactions that we have with each other; We learn and play together: We learn how to live and we develop our cognitive and social skills.

Positive Socialization (Write below some positive socialization)	Negative Socialization (write below some negative socialization)
Eg. We eat together Eg. We encourage and motivate others	Eg. We drink ourselves into a stupor eg. we gossip and promote stereotypes

Draw:

Why do we need socialization?

Write eight sentences explaining why we need socialization.

Do you think socialization is very important to our survival as a species? Why or why not?

ISOLATION

Define Isolation:

What would happen if someone were isolated? Research case of Feral Children and send us your research at www.childrenliveon.net

Brainstorm

Steps To A Healthy Me & Self Responsibility

Auset Atenra

Self-Isolation:

What is self-isolation?

Is self-isolation essential in helping one when one comes of age and is searching for one's own Self truth?

Research people like yogis, sages who practice self-isolations.

Why do they self isolate?

Making Friends

Define Friends:

Why do we need friends?

Questions:

1. What kind of friend am I?

2. How do I choose my friends?

3. How do I resolve conflict with my friend?

4. What is peer pressure?

TO DO:

1. **Write an advertisement to get a new friend.**

(submit on www.childrenliveon.net)

2. **Create a slogan defining the criteria for a friend.**

(submit on www.childrenliveon.net)

Steps To A Healthy Me & Self Responsibility   Auset Atenra

Peer Pressure

What is Peer Pressure?

Peer Pressure

PEER PRESSURE SKIT

Write a skit. Create a situation where peer pressure is the theme you role-play. Create two endings, one active and one inactive; one ending in which the main character has high self-esteem and is a creative leader. The other ending in which a person has a low self-esteem, where the character follows the crowd rather than to think independently.

Commercial 30 seconds -1 minute

Life moves in spirals and circles with each species expressing its individuality yet at the same time connecting in oneness to support the balance of life.

"Out Of Many We Are One". Out of One Came Many"

Create a commercial explaining why stereotypes, prejudice and discrimination are destructive to the unity of Self.

If someone dares you to steal from a store, you want to fit in with the crowd but stealing goes against your moral and better judgment. What do you do?

Steps To A Healthy Me & Self Responsibility   Auset Atenra

Hug Page

Write the names of your friends, family members, classmates. Next to their names write something nice about them.

Draw or paste photos of hugs:

Steps To A Healthy Me & Self Responsibility

Prejudice & Discrimination

What are stereotypes?

Discuss with your group how stereotypes are harmful

Create scenarios of stereotypes, prejudice and discrimination.

Discuss ways you can avoid using stereotypes.

What is the difference between prejudice, stereotype and discrimination?

Write below examples of each:

Stereotype	Discrimination	Prejudice
Meaning:	Meaning:	Meaning:

Steps To A Healthy Me & Self Responsibility   Auset Atenra

Write a Persuasive speech on why discrimination and prejudice harm's everyone.

Post your video on www.childrenliveon.net

Diversity is what makes the world so beautiful and colorful. From one source we see myriads of creation. How boring life would be if we didn't have diversity.

"Out Of Many We Are One". Out of One Came Many"

Role Models

ROLE MODEL

Think of someone you know who practices self-awareness. Write down 5 or more things that you like about them.

What can you emulate or learn from this person?

Who do you admire? Who do you want to be more like?

Draw or Paste a picture of the person you admire.

Steps To A Healthy Me & Self Responsibility   Auset Atenra

Leadership & Self Responsibility Tips

Michael Bland Principal (BARACK OBAMA MALE LEADERSHIP ACADEMY)

Use these Tips as an affirmation: **Repeat Daily**

o I will set High Expectations

o I will Find a Safe Haven and an environment where education is valued.

o I will Learn how to prioritize what's important to me

o I will practice Looking at the consequences of my actions and my choices before I make them.

o I will choose choices that will not be detrimental to me.

o Knowing my value system will help me navigate through difficult choices.

o I will participate in extracurricular activities.

o Goal Setting will allow me to stay on track

o I will learn life lessons from the people and the environment around me.

o I see equity in my education, my education is an investment in my future

"WHEN YOU EMPOWER CHILDREN IN WHO THEY ARE AND WHAT ROLE THEY PLAY IN THE INSTRUCTION AND LEARNING THAT TAKE PLACE THEIR LEADERSHIP QUALITIES START TO COME OUT. LET'S PROVIDE CHILDREN WITH A STRONG FAMILY STRUCTURE IN THE HOME, SCHOOL AND COMMUNITY."

MICHAEL BLAND (PRINCIPAL)

WHAT IS LEADERSHIP?

Qualities of a great Leader (write some qualities)	Write the name of Leaders with these qualities
Respect for others	
Commitment to the cause	
Creativity	
Passion and enthusiasm	
A sense of humor	
Trustworthy & Righteous	

Leadership Roles

Roles/Duties of a Leader	Take Action: How can you use these leadership skills? Start by creating a plan and write it below.
Create a plan	
Keep the group on the task at hand	
Help and support others in their group	
Evaluate Progress	
Find solutions	
Teach and inspire others	
Time management: Keep track of time	
Help others to develop their leadership skills	

Draw:

Steps To A Healthy Me & Self Responsibility

Time Capsule –

Worries, fear, memories, tears, laughter

Create a time capsule and place all your worries, fears, memories happy/sad, laughter, Love inspirations inside. Open it in six months: how has your philosophy changed? The things that worry you, does it still seem significant?

FEAR	WORRIES	MEMORIES *FUNNY:* *SCARY:* Happy	TEARS	LAUGHTER *What brings you laughter?*

LAUGH OUT LOUD

Practice laughing everyday!

Whenever we want to learn or do something we practice it.

Why don't we practice laughing?

Laughter is a healing remedy.

LAUGH!!!

Laughter is a healing remedy.

Research and find where someone uses laughter, a sunny disposition, or positive Thought Reinforcement to heal one's self or overcome difficulties.

How can laughter help me?

How can having a balanced viewpoint affect my quality of life?

I challenge you, my friend, to a daily laughter exercise!

Fear

What is the difference between fear and phobia?

Do you think we can live our lives without fear?

Draw:

Steps To A Healthy Me & Self Responsibility   Auset Atenra

FEAR AWARENESS:

Ignorance is the root of all fear. The goal here is to bring awareness to the effect of our fears. How can we successfully master how our fears demonstrate its sneaky little powers over our lives? If we observe our fears and the fears of others, then we can learn how to redirect our thoughts to the root of our fears. We can master what we manifest into our world.

If we are in immediate danger Fear is also a tool that can protect us from danger so perhaps one can't really be free from all fears.

Remember what the "law of attraction says" whatever we spend our time and energy on, we bring it into our world. Therefore, the things that we spend our time worrying about we are also bringing it into our world. We create many of our fears by the things we imagine.

Lack of knowledge is the root of all FEARS. If we know then there is no need to fear. Fear arises out of our ignorance. The only way to master fear is through KNOWING. Through knowing we become free from all fears.

DO YOU AGREE OR DISAGREE?

We spend our lives worrying about so many things that would have never happened if we didn't worry about them so much.

What is your thought on this premise?

WHAT AM I AFRAID OF?

Draw:

How can I understand fear?

Can one be free from all fears?

Understanding Fear Requires Us To Look It In The Face.

It is very important to understand fear, because if we don't, we will take it with us into our future without understanding the reason behind the fear. Looking at fear allows us to shatter the illusion to see 'what is'?

Fear- poses a threat to our life. danger	Phobia- feelings of treat but in reality poses little or no actual danger	Cause Reason for your fear; what triggers your fear?	Effect How does it affect your life?	Shatter Illusion- What is reveal, hidden underneath 'The Truth'

Did the thing that you worry about come through?

Was it worth the worry?

Did worrying about it make it better?

AFFIRMATION

I am on the path of Self Knowing.

I eradicate all my ignorance and Fear with "SELF TRUTH"

I transform worries into healing energy and goal achievement.

Inhale exhale. I am calm. I put my healing circle on

I am protected and nothing can harm me. I Am Safe.

I Am Happy. I Am Peaceful. I Am Calm. I Am All.

Draw:

LOVE

What is Love?

What is Unconditional Love?

Research: SELF LOVE

SELF-LOVE:

I ACCEPT MYSELF at this level – I Am That I Am.

I have the power to Infinite Possibility – I Am That I Will to Be

I love myself enough to cultivate HEALTHY HABITS.

I LOVE myself ENOUGH to cultivate HEALTHY MIND

I Love myself enough to cultivate HEALTHY WAY OF LIFE

I Love myself enough to cultivate HEALTHY RELATIONSHIPS

Sick Minds

This is a touchy subject and nobody wants to talk about it. Mind sickness is prevalent in life as a result of the duality nature of the world's existence. Many bad and negative thoughts arise from the minds of all beings. Therefore we must constantly be practicing Thoughts Awareness and Stillness. And do **NOT** drink alcohol and take drugs.

❖ Many beings suffer mind sickness and will do evil things.

❖ Remember to practice daily stillness and discernment

❖ Talk to someone you trust if others approach you with evil intentions.

Children because of the duality nature of life, evil exists. Therefore, there are sick beings in the world, deceiving and conniving; mind controlling and spellbinding; these predators prey on the naive, vulnerable and children. Be aware and stay safe. Protect your body, mind and self. Be healed and be sovereign.

Remember: Your body is a sacred temple.

Guard and protect it.   STAY SAFE.

Much Reverence. Much Honor To I And I.

Most importantly
REMEMBER!!!!

Talk to your parents or someone you trust if someone is pressuring you for inappropriate behaviors.

Talk to your parents or someone you trust if an adult is making inappropriate gestures to you, more than likely this is the initiation of them planning something evil.

Remember: This is a duality world. Evil and Purity exist. Stay in Self Awareness and Keep your MIND Pure.

I Bow To I And I In Self, Light And Truth.

Daily Practice

REMEMBER:

THIS IS THE MOMENT!

- ✔ BE PRESENT IN THE MOMENT
- ✔ STAY ALERT
- ✔ STAY STILL WITHOUT THOUGHTS
- ✔ SMILE – LIFE IS A SACRED GAME
- ✔ CONSCIOUS BREATHING
- ✔ SELF AWARENESS
- ✔ BE IN COMMAND OF YOUR MIND

COMPASSION

What is compassion?

How can I show compassion towards the suffering of others?

Steps To A Healthy Me & Self Responsibility

QUESTIONS TO ASK ONESELF

Who am I?

Where did I come from?

Why am I here?

What is my Self Purpose?

How Am I Responding to Life?

Am I responding to life with Self Awareness?

Where am I going after I shed this body?

How do I get there?

My Ideas:

What do I know about life?

What is my experience of life?

Stepping Stones

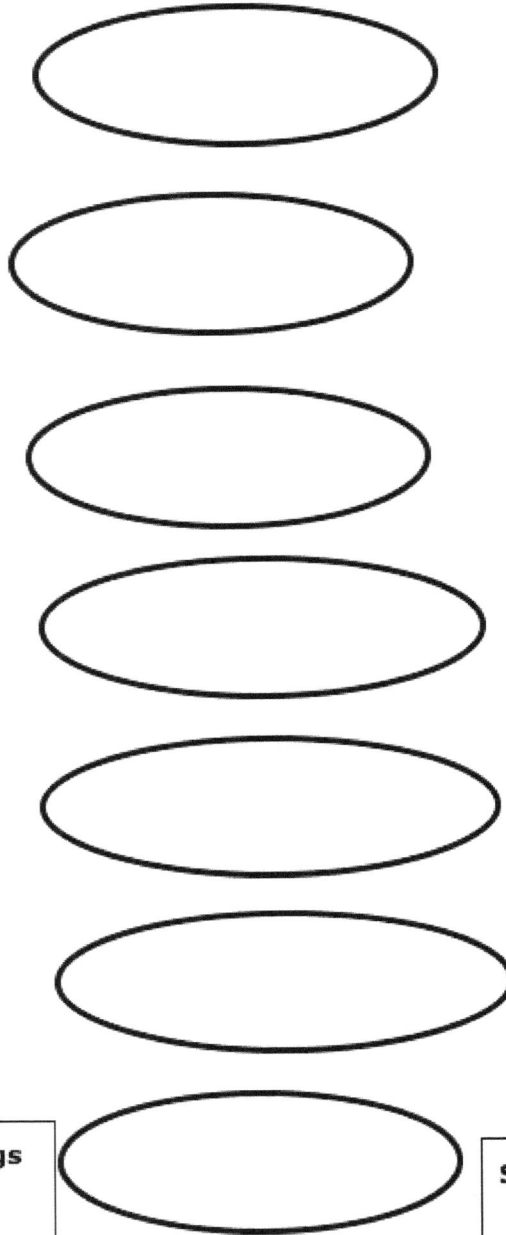

What action, events or things do you think will be helpful to attain your goal?

Eg. To get to a car you must take lessons and pass the test. Sometime you might have to do something you don't like to achieve what you want

I accept my responsibilities and I with conscious Awareness will do what is needed to be done.

Stepping stones are needed to get you from where you are now to your destination/goals

I was once working a delivery job I didn't like but it was a stepping stone for me, just to help me pay my bills until I get what I wanted.

GOALS

What are my goals? short term? long term? What are the Steps To Achieve My Goals? On a construction sheet of paper recreate your goal chart.

GOALS CHART

Short-term Goals	Steps To Achieving goal	Did I achieve my goal? How long did it take?	Long Term Goals	Steps To Achieving Goals	Did I achieve my goal? How long did it take?

Guiding Principles of Self

I _____ _is thriving for Self-responsibility, Self-mastery, self-awareness, self-identity, self-preservation, self-discipline, self control, self-innovation and self-actualization.

SELF-RESPONSIBILITY: I have the ability to respond with Self Awareness. Conscious breath, thoughts, words and actions. I am responsible for my actions, my life , my education, my health, and my self balance.

SELF-MASTERY-   I am that I Am. I Am that I will be.   In this awareness I know my given skills, knowledge and abilities. I utilize them appropriately.

SELF-AWARENESS: I am mindful of my thoughts, words, feelings, and actions. My thoughts, my words, my feelings, and my actions create my reality. I am Pure Light.

SELF-PRESERVATION: I strive to maintain balance of mind, body, and self. I protect myself from destructive and negative thoughts and words, food that promotes premature death. I thrive on actions that promote longevity. Life is for living. I Am alive. I live in harmony and balance with my One True Pure Self.

SELF-IDENTITY: I practice "Who Am I Self Inquiry" Meditation so I can know who I am for myself. I Must know for myself who I am.   I Am All. I must realize that All is myself. I express myself through nature. I express my Authentic Self .I am That I Am. I Am That Has No Name. I Am That Can't Be Explained.

SELF-DISCIPLINE: I check and manage my own behavior, therefore, someone else or a system won't discipline or manage me. I Am in command of my mind and my body.

SELF-CONTROL: I am the master of my feelings and mind. He who conquers ego self is the mightiest warrior. My actions are my karma. I am in command. Mind Be Still. I Am the Self.

SELF-INNOVATION: I am a creator, creating. I use my creative power to create with my thoughts, my words, my hands, my actions and my knowledge. What are my thoughts creating me? What will my hand's creation be? What will my footprints leave?

SELF Kno: Be Who I Am. I am Primal Light. All Is Myself. I Am One With All. I am balanced. I Am That I Am. . I Am That I Will Be.   I am self aligned with I One True Pure Self.

SELF-LOVE: I Love myself enough to connect to my inner Truth and live from that awareness.   I live my best life in equanimity and harmony. .   I Am That I Am.

Books author recommend

The 16 Habits of Mind

Learning and Leading with Habits of Mind:
16 Essential Characteristics for Success
Edited by Arthur L. Costa & Bena Kallick

Habits of Mind is knowing how to behave intelligently when you DON'T know the answer. It means having a disposition toward behaving intelligently when confronted with problems, the answers to which are not immediately known: dichotomies, dilemmas, enigmas and uncertainties.

Our focus is on performance under challenging conditions that demand strategic reasoning, insightfulness, perseverance, creativity, and craftsmanship. The critical attribute of intelligent human beings is not only having information, but also knowing how to act on it. Employing Habits of Mind requires drawing forth certain patterns of intellectual behavior that produce powerful results. They are a composite of many skills, attitudes and proclivities.

The 16 Habits of Mind identified by Costa and Kallick include:

- Persisting
- Thinking and communicating with clarity and precision
- Managing impulsivity
- Gathering data through all senses
- Listening with understanding and empathy
- Creating, imagining, innovating
- Thinking flexibly
- Responding with wonderment and awe
- Thinking about thinking (metacognition)
- Taking responsible risks
- Striving for accuracy
- Finding humor
- Questioning and posing problems
- Thinking interdependently
- Applying past knowledge to new situations
- Remaining open to continuous learning

Glossary

Virtue:

LEADERSHIP: To show the way; guide or cause other to follow you; to direct

Self-discipline: the ability to motivate oneself in spite of a negative emotional state. Qualities associated with self-discipline include willpower, hard work and persistence.

Self-Awareness

Self-Awareness is the ability to be aware of your emotions, thoughts, feelings, actions, personality and character.

Philosophy

Philosophy is your ideas about life, the way you think about life, people. What is your philosophy on life?

Motivation

Motivation is the force that draws you to move towards something.

"Learning isn't about being smart enough, It's about being motivated enough" Marilyn Ferguson

What inspires you to complete a task when you don't feel like it? What is your motivation?

NEED VS WANT

Need is necessary for survival,

Wants is something you can live without.

Purpose vs Meaning

Purpose is what you are born to do, as an apple tree is destined to bare apples.

Meaning is the significance, or importance we attach to something or someone.

Self-control- is the ability to control one's emotion, desire, or action by one's own will.

Emotional Awareness

Emotions is a heightened sense of awareness of electrical fields of Energy that extends inward and outward of the realm of our body. It can pick up sensations we are not aware of and then it feeds them into the brain, the brain sends signals to our body, based on our previous programing of our mind. We will react based on that sensation. Sometimes we don't fully understand the emotions we are feeling. Our interpretations and expressions might reflect quite the contrary. I have had many overwhelming emotions that I was unaware of the root cause or the trigger.

Chemicals that trigger emotions are also created in the brain. The way that I feel about something triggers an emotion, If I change my thoughts and feelings I can master my emotions. If I practice emotional awareness then I can learn the triggers, and understand when I have an overwhelming emotion to pause and meditate on the root cause and the road to healing.

We have to try to get to the root of the emotions only then can we be free and be healed. Only then will we become the masters of our emotions.

Remember we all must face our demons. We cannot run away and hide, we cannot drown ourselves in the negative and destructive creations like drugs, alcohol, promiscuity etc, we will only feed the demon and our troubles will escalate. We have to get to the root cause of all our emotions to heal and be whole.

How can I practice Emotional Awareness?

Emotions are generated in the brain. The brain is the engine of the body. The brain informs the body of what to do.

We view life based on our perspective of things, It is our perspective, how we view things that upsets us, and not the things."

- first we think,
- then we feel,
- and then we act.

What is the difference between emotions and feelings?

"Emotions are the raw material. They come with the DNA package.

Feelings are the interpretation of the raw data given by the brain and reinforced by the individual's culture."

Jack Block, Ph.D. Professor of psychology at UC Berkeley and the director of the Block

Project, a longitudinal study of child development

Birthday:

Elements:

Character Traits:

Zodiac Sign:

Chinese Sign:

Kemet Sign:

ZODIAC

Aries

(March 21 - April 19)
Full of fun and fire, Aries is the first sign of the zodiac, and so thrives on being number one. Aries kids are confident, brave and filled with moxy and drive. These kids love to win and are always on the lookout for their next adventure. Keep them happy by keeping them active and on the move.

Taurus

(April 20 - May 20)
Taurus kids are calm and peaceful and love to spend time in nature. These earthy Bulls of the zodiac know exactly what they want and how to get it. You'll often find them either out in the woods or at home getting comfortable. Let them move at their own pace as they can resist when they are rushed.

Gemini

(May 21 - June 20)
This airy sign stands out for its quick wit, intelligence and ability to talk, talk and talk some more. Curious and information hungry, the sign of the Twins has lots of questions and is always seeking answers. Friendly Gemini kids like to keep busy and thrive on social interactions and mental stimulation. Give them a word game to play and watch them win!

Cancer

(June 21 - July 22)
Moon-ruled Cancer kids are gentle, imaginative and wise. Powered by the Crab, this sign likes to get to know you before they let you in on all the treasures they hold inside. Loyal to friends and family, Cancer is a warm and soothing presence in any environment. When they get plenty of food and rest, they are at their best.

Leo

(July 23 - August 22)
Leo the Lion is known for its warm and generous heart. Playful and outgoing, Leo likes to live large and enjoy life. This astro kid enjoys performing, socializing and playing games of any kind. Able to create a fun environment almost anywhere, Leo is a popular and engaging playmate. Give them a way to show their pride and watch them shine!

Virgo

(August 23 - September 22)
Earthy Virgo is smart, grounded and skilled at making things work. Give this crafty sign a project to do and watch how much detail and care they put into it. Virgo kids love learning how the world works and are always looking for new ways to improve on existing models. Keep them busy with an important job or task and see how they thrive!

Libra

(September 23 - October 22)

Lovely Libra is charming, easygoing and diplomatic. This airy sign loves to spend time hanging out with friends and socializing. Fashionable and artistic, Libra kids have a gift for making everything around them just a little more beautiful. They do the best when they are in a calm, peaceful and soothing environment surrounded by people they enjoy spending time wit

Scorpio

(October 23 - November 21)

Private and powerful, Scorpio kids love to get to the bottom of things. This watery sign has an ability to be a loyal and trusted friend and is known for its wise and thoughtful advice. Scorpios aren't fooled easily and appreciate honesty and a straightforward approach, since they don't miss much about people, places or things. Give this astro kid a mystery to solve and watch them go!

Sagittarius

(November 22 - December 21)

Carefree, optimistic and cheerful, Sagittarius kids know how to enjoy life. These fire signs love to meet new people and see new places and are always seeking out their next adventure. Sagittarius' enjoy storytelling and cracking jokes and can spend hours laughing with friends and having fun. They love a chance to share what they know, and are natural teachers and educators.

Capricorn

(December 22 - January 19)

The sign of the Goat knows how to make just about anything useful. Depend on Capricorn kids to take charge, manage and take care of seemingly challenging projects and jobs, for they will have them mastered in no time! This practical sign is patient and steady and not easily distracted from the things that matter to them. Treat Capricorns with respect and notice how they blossom.

Aquarius

(January 20 - February 18)

Quirky and inventive Aquarius always seems to have something new to share. This friendly air sign thrives on the unusual and is attracted to anything that is just a little bit shocking or surprising. Aquarius kids need to feel like it's ok to be exactly who they are, no matter how outside the box they might appear.

Pisces

(February 19 - March 20)

Gentle and kind, Pisces kids love to have the chance to dream and explore their imaginations freely. This creative water sign is a natural artist, filled to the brim with inspiration and whimsy. Pisces also enjoys spending time in nature, particularly at the ocean. Support this special sign by periodically giving them ample opportunity to wander and drift, without a set timeline or plan.

AUTOGRAPH: Have family, teachers and friends sign your book with advice or compliment.

AUTOGRAPH: Have family, teachers and friends sign your book with advice or compliment.

Steps To My True Self

A Self Awareness Guide book for Youth

Steps To A Healthy Me & Self Responsibility

Theme: Self Awareness

Steps To My True Self Book 2

Steps To My Inner Purpose & Creativity

Theme: Self Realization

GROWING MY INSIDE STRONG

Being Who I Am – Being/creating in balance and harmony

Theme: Self Affirmations and Meditations

Many human beings have a hard time balancing their feelings, their minds and choosing the right actions.   "Growing My Inside Strong" workbook explores "Steps To A Healthy Self and Self Responsibility. Children learn that sometimes our mind tells us to do things that are not right, therefore we should NOT do everything our mind tells us.   I am in command of my mind. "MIND BE STILL". I am in command.

Here I can Learn techniques to balance and manage one's own mind, Feelings and Creations. How to come to self realization and choose to be a decent noble and Balanced Human Being? Learn Techniques to dissolve the ego false self and return to "Self Truth".

About the author

Auset Maat is Self-Knowing in the Human Avatar. I mission is to share "Stillness & Self Inquiry" with All The I and I.

"OUT OF ONE CAME MANY".   All Is Myself. I Am One With All.

 I Bow To I and I In Self, Light And Truth. I Enjoy Traveling To Share Stillness & Healing Sound Vibrations

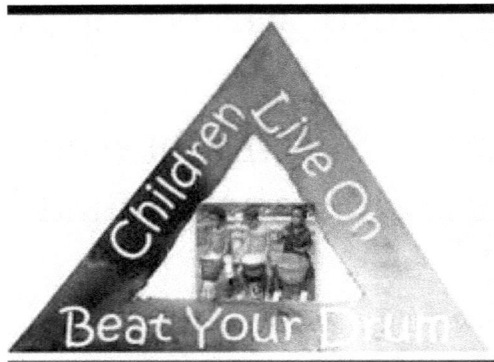

www.ingramcontent.com/pod-product-compliance
Lightning Source LLC
Chambersburg PA
CBHW062040090426

42740CB00016B/2964